KT-379-075

COUNTRY FACT FILES

RUSSIA

John Sallnow
and Tatyana Saiko

MACDONALD YOUNG BOOKS

First published in 1996 y Macdonald Young Books
an imprint of Wayland Publishers Ltd
© Macdonald Young Books 1996

Macdonald Young Books
61 Western Road
Hove
East Sussex
BN3 1JD

Design and typesetting Roger Kohn Designs
Editor Diana Russell
Picture research Valerie Mulcahy
Illustration János Márffy
Commissioning editor Debbie Fox

We are grateful to the following for permission
to reproduce photographs:
Front Cover: Tatyana Saiko *above,*
SCR Photo Library/David Toase *below;*
B & C Alexander, pages 17 *above*, 37 *above*; Ardea London
Ltd, pages 39 *below* (J M Labat), 41 (Ferrero/Labat); The
Associated Press Ltd, page 13 (Misha Japaridze); Colorific!,
page 15 (Bob Krist/Black Star); The Environmental Picture
Library, pages 11 (Pierre Gleizes), 39 *above* (Mark Warford);
JVZ, page 19 (Eugene Poggeo); Novosti (London), pages 12
above, 16, 26 *above* (Dmitri Donskoy), 26 *below*, 30/31, 33;
Rex Features Ltd, page 43 *below* (R Roderni White); SCR
Photo Library, pages 23 and 43 *above* (David Toase); Tatyana
Saiko, pages 34, 42; Frank Spooner Pictures/GAMMA, pages
27 *below* (A Hernandez/Liaison), 29 (Hires-Merillon), 35
(Swersey/Liaison); Tony Stone Images, pages 8/9 and 24
above (Gavin Hellier); Sygma, pages 14 and 20 (Jacques
Langevin), 24 *below* (Epix), 28 (Sparonenkov), 30
(J P Laffont); Sygma Paris, page 32; Travel Ink, pages 12
below and 18/19 (David Toase), 25 (Life File/Oleg
Svyatoslavsky); TRIP, pages 17 *below* (V Larionov), 21 (Bob
Turner), 22 *above* (F Torrance), 22 *below* (M Kenkin), 27
above (V Kanashev), 36 (A Kuznetsov), 37 *below* (Bob
Turner); Zefa, pages 8 (G Steemans), 18, 38 (Dr Hans
Kramarz); Viktor Zhivotchenko, page 10/11.

The statistics given in this book are the most up to date
available at the time of going to press

Printed in Hong Kong by Wing King Tong

A CIP catalogue record for this book is available from
the British Library

ISBN: 0 7500 1969 7

Special thanks to the children of School no. 599,
Tushinskiy District, North West Region, Moscow,
who are pictured on the front cover.

UNIVERSITY OF
CENTRAL ENGLAND

BOOK NO. 30253950
SUBJECT NO. 914.7/Sal

INFORMATION SERVICES

C
O
N
T
E
N
T
S

Words that are explained in the glossary are printed in
SMALL CAPITALS the first time they are mentioned in the text.

◼ INTRODUCTION

The Russian Federation is the largest country in the world and has the sixth biggest population. It is so vast that it would be possible to fit the territory of Great Britain into the Federation 74 times – and still have a little space left over. The country straddles the two continents of Europe and Asia, stretching from the Baltic Sea to the shores of the Pacific Ocean.

The Federation is also known as "Russia", a term that comes from the ancient name of "Rus". For centuries, Russia was ruled by the TSARS, until they were overthrown in the COMMUNIST Russian Revolution of 1917. This was followed by a period of civil war. From 1922 to 1991, Russia was part of the Soviet Union, which was a banding together of 15 republics that were usually known as Soviet Socialist Republics – hence the alternative title of Union of Soviet Socialist Republics (USSR).

For many years, the Soviet Union and the USA were rival "superpowers", and there was strong competition between them.

▲ *This extended family (including uncles, aunts, grandparents, cousins) lives in traditionally decorated wooden houses in a village in southern Siberia. Living conditions here can be poor – for example, village roads are often not paved, but just consist of bare earth, and the houses may not have a piped water supply.*

However, today the USSR no longer exists and respect and co-operation have replaced rivalry. Russia has taken the former Soviet Union's seat at world organizations such as the United Nations, and it still has much influence in world political affairs.

Since 1991, the country has undergone rapid and dramatic changes, which have affected all aspects of life there. In this book, you can find out what Russia is like today. You will read about the country's varied landscape and climate, its wealth

▼ *Trinity and St Sergius, Russia's largest monastery, was built in the Moscow region in the 16th century. Today it is the chief centre of the Russian Orthodox Church.*

RUSSIA AT A GLANCE

- Area: 17,075,400 square kilometres
- Population (1995 estimate): 148,300,000
- Population density (1995): 8.7 people per sq km
- Capital: Moscow (called Moskva in Russian), population 8,793,000
- Other main cities: St Petersburg 4.9 million; Novosibirsk 1.4 million
- Highest mountain: Mount Elbrus, 5,642 metres
- Longest river: Lena, 4,400 kilometres
- Language: Russian
- Major religion: Russian Orthodox (Islam in some republics)
- Life expectancy (1994): 57 years for men; 71 years for women
- Currency: Rouble, written as R
- Economy: Rapid move to market economy and PRIVATIZATION since January 1992
- Major resources: oil, natural gas, coal, iron ore, copper, gold, nickel, silver, tungsten, diamonds, uranium (but much overlain by PERMAFROST)
- Major products: aircraft, lorries, cars, tractors, combine harvesters, scientific goods, cameras, timber products, wooden dolls, caviar, vodka
- Environmental problems: still suffering effects of world's worst nuclear accident in 1986 at Chernobyl (now in independent Ukraine), pollution of water courses, rivers and lakes by oil seepage, careless use of chemical fertilizers in agriculture

of natural resources, the make-up of its population, how people go about their daily lives and how the country is governed. You will also read about the country's agriculture, trade and industry, its transport facilities, its environmental advantages and problems, and the prospect for Russia's future in the 21st century.

THE LANDSCAPE

Russia can be divided into several physical regions. The European part runs from the Baltic Sea in the west to the Ural mountains in the east, while the south includes the mountainous slopes of the north Caucasus. The Arctic islands and coasts have cold, polar "deserts" and a treeless landscape known as TUNDRA. To the south, this is replaced by vast coniferous forests called TAIGA, which cover large areas in Europe, central Siberia and the Far East. The southern part of the European plain and west Siberia have open grasslands known as STEPPES. The great size of the country means that vast belts or zones of vegetation continue for hundreds and thousands of kilometres.

In the northern European area, there is dense coniferous forest, which gives way to mixed and deciduous forest to the south. The steppes have a very rich soil, called CHERNOZEM, or "black earth", because of its colour. The Caucasus mountain range varies in height between 800 and more than 5,000 metres. It lies between the Black Sea and the Caspian Sea and forms the southern border of European Russia. In these southern regions, there are areas of semi-desert, and even a desert in Kalmykia.

The Urals are less rugged than the Caucasus, with an average height of around 1,000 metres. There are several natural passes between

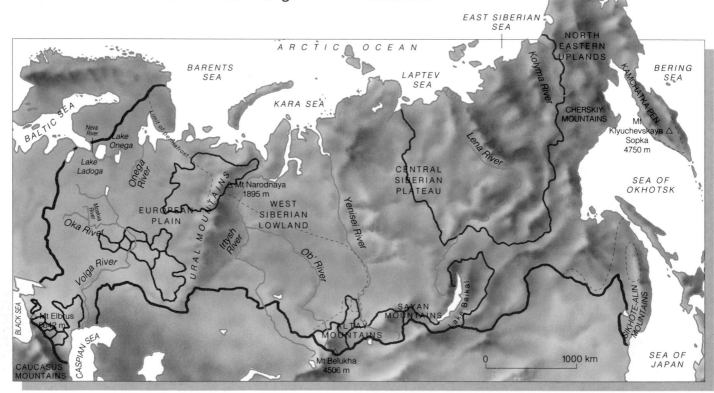

◀ *At 4,750 m, Klyuchevskaya Sopka is Eurasia's highest active volcano. Located in Russia's Kamchatka Peninsula, it has erupted 10 times since 1945, most recently in 1991.*

the mountains. The highest peak in the Urals is Mount Narodnaya in the north, at 1,895 metres. The range forms the boundary between the two continents of Europe and Asia, so that Russia is one-quarter in Europe but three-quarters in Asia.

To the east of the Urals lie Siberia and the Far East. The western part of Siberia is a huge lowland which stretches 1,600 km across and 2,400 km from north to south, making it the largest plain in the world. It is a vast frozen area in winter and a gigantic marshland in summer. It also contains large deposits of oil and natural gas.

East Siberia and the Far East contain several mountain ranges, in between which

KEY FACTS

● Russia's River Volga is the longest river in Europe (3,690 km).
● Russia measures 9,000 km from east to west, and 4,000 km from north to south.
● The country covers 11 time zones. Before people in Moscow have sat down to lunch, those in eastern Siberia have already gone to bed.
● Russia's largest lake is Baikal in Siberia, covering 31,500 sq km and containing one-fifth of the world's freshwater resources.

▼ *The European taiga is part of a massive zone of coniferous forest. This is Pechora National Park in Komi republic.*

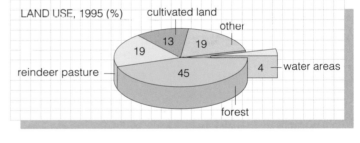

LAND USE, 1995 (%)

cultivated land
other
13 19
19
reindeer pasture
45   4 — water areas
forest

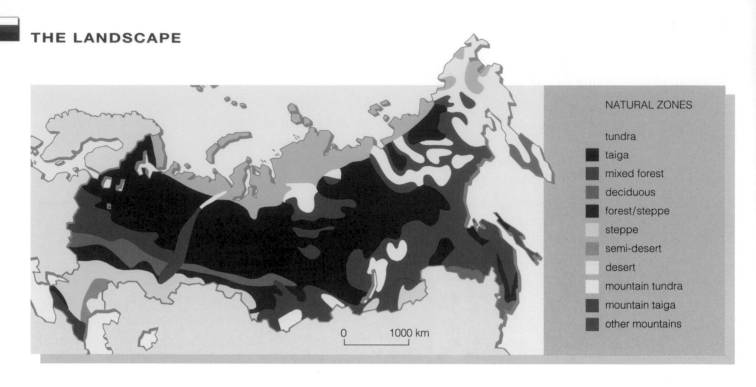

NATURAL ZONES

tundra
taiga
mixed forest
deciduous
forest/steppe
steppe
semi-desert
desert
mountain tundra
mountain taiga
other mountains

0   1000 km

flow some of the longest rivers in the world, such as the Lena (4,400 km), the Irtysh (4,248 km) and the Yenisei (4,102 km). The natural vegetation here is the taiga forest, consisting of larch, spruce and pine, below which lies the permafrost. This is permanently frozen ground, which can be up to 800 metres thick. Only the upper 20–150 centimetres thaw out during the summer. Most of the permafrost has not thawed out since the last Ice Age. Bones of woolly mammoths are often found here — and sometimes even a whole baby mammoth.

▼ *Baikal, the world's deepest lake (1,637m). This rock on the shore of the lake is called "Two Brothers".*

◄ *Russians call Europe's longest river "Mother Volga". It has been a key transport route for 1,000 years. This is its junction with the River Oka, near Nizhniy Novgorod.*

CLIMATE AND WEATHER

▲ *Encouraged by "Father Frost", a young "walrus" braves New Year temperatures of −15°C for the air and 1–2°C for the water.*

As Russia is such a large country, there are major variations in its climate. But generally it has long, cold winters and warm or hot summers. This climate is very different from that of the UK, but similar to parts of the USA. In January, most of Russia has temperatures below zero, and there is a "pole of cold" in north-eastern Siberia. The coldest city on Earth is Verkhoyansk; near here the world's lowest temperature (apart from Antarctica) was recorded at −71°C. In Siberia and the Far East, when the temperature falls to −40°C children do not have to go to school; in the European part of Russia, including Moscow, it does not get as cold as this, so here children are excused going to school when the temperature reaches −30°C. Only on the Black Sea coast are January temperatures in cities above freezing point.

In July, all of Russia has warm or hot temperatures – up to 35°C at the "winter pole of cold" at Verkhoyansk. This city has the greatest temperature range of anywhere in the world: more than 100°C.

Russians love to sunbathe and swim even in winter. River ice is removed and people swim in the cold water; they are known as "walruses". Many believe their icy swim helps to prevent them becoming ill in the long Russian winter.

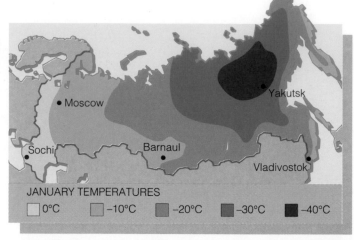

JANUARY TEMPERATURES

☐ 0°C　☐ –10°C　■ –20°C　■ –30°C　■ –40°C

KEY FACTS

● 16% of Russia's territory lies inside the Arctic Circle.

● Average temperatures in Russia range from –1° to –50°C in January, and from 1° to 25°C in July.

● Average January temperatures in Vladivostok are 30°C less than in Nice (France), although both cities are on the same latitude.

● Siberia has an average 40–50 cm of snow a year, while the Arctic north of European Russia has an average of 70–80 cm.

● Although the Black Sea coast is still popular with Russian holiday-makers, rising prices mean that it is now sometimes cheaper for them to holiday in Cyprus instead.

▲ *North of the Arctic Circle, the ocean and rivers are frozen for more than 6 months of the year. Ships can easily become trapped in ice here.*

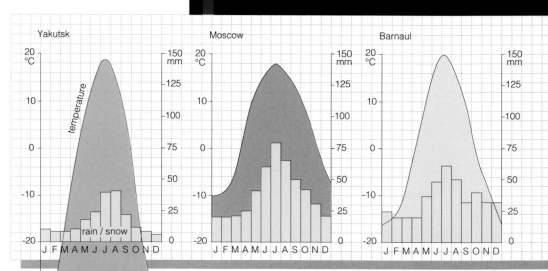

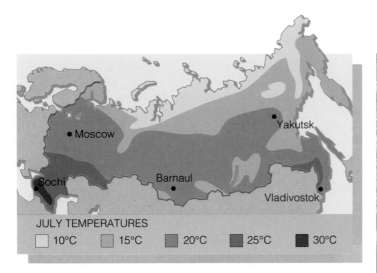

JULY TEMPERATURES

☐ 10°C ☐ 15°C ▨ 20°C ▨ 25°C ■ 30°C

▶ *Many people spend sunny weekends at city beaches. These sunbathers are relaxing on Peter and Paul Island at the mouth of the Neva, St Petersburg.*

In Siberia, summer is short and winter quickly returns at the beginning of September, while in European Russia there is more gradual change during September and October. Moscow's first snow normally comes in November and the five months of winter then dominate the weather. In the northern parts of Siberia, winter lasts for up to nine months.

At Yakutsk in the Russian Far East, temperatures are below freezing for seven months of the year, compared to six months at Barnaul in east Siberia and four and a half months in Moscow. The same period of freezing temperatures is found at Vladivostok on the Pacific Ocean. The city of Sochi on the Black Sea has daytime temperatures above freezing all year and its annual rainfall distribution reflects its Mediterranean-type climate.

Moscow and Barnaul have maximum rainfall in summer, notably in July, while in Vladivostok the maximum occurs in August and September; this can be accompanied by tropical cyclones and typhoons from the Sea of Japan. Total annual rain and snowfall here can reach 1,000 mm. In contrast, Yakutsk has relatively little rain or snow; while in the steppe and semi-desert zones, there is little moisture all year round. Areas around the Caspian Sea may have less than 150 mm of rain a year. Droughts and hot winds are common.

This great range in climate and weather means that Russian people have to adapt their lives accordingly. For instance, in the winter they take advantage of powerful central heating systems at home, and dress themselves in furs when they go outside.

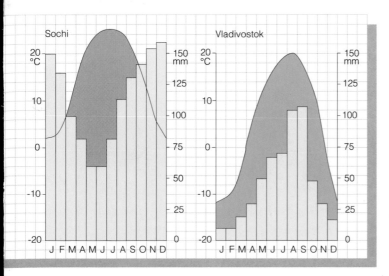

■ NATURAL RESOURCES

Russia has a vast wealth of natural resources, with deposits of every known useful mineral. It is the world's largest producer of natural gas and nickel and is the third largest producer of oil and coal. It is also the world's second largest producer of diamonds, after Australia, with 1994 production of 17 million carats. And it is the world's largest producer of asbestos, with 800,000 tonnes mined in 1994.

Many of the minerals are found in Siberia and the Far East, where approximately 63% of territory is underlain by permafrost. Powerful steam hoses are used to melt it, which adds to the cost of extracting the mineral ores. Iron ore is found in the Kursk region and aluminium ores in the north of European Russia. For centuries, the Ural mountains have been exploited for their rich resources of copper, iron, molybdenum, chrome and precious stones. This is still an important mining and industrial centre.

In the mid-1980s, Russia was the world's largest producer of iron and steel; today, it is the third largest producer of pig iron, at

KEY FACTS

● Russia's total coal reserves are estimated at more than 5,000 billion tonnes, of which 3,500 billion are in the Tunguska-Lena basin.
● Much of Russia's oil and natural gas is exported to West Europe, and is used to pay for food imports.
● Russia has the largest reserves of coniferous timber in the world – 64.8 billion cubic metres.
● In 1993, 12% of total electric energy was generated by nuclear power.
● Russia has reserves of about 160 billion tonnes of peat, or 60% of the world's total – mainly located in west Siberia.

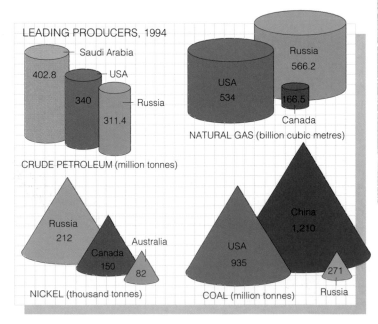

LEADING PRODUCERS, 1994

Saudi Arabia 402.8
USA 340
Russia 311.4

CRUDE PETROLEUM (million tonnes)

Russia 566.2
USA 534
Canada 166.5

NATURAL GAS (billion cubic metres)

Russia 212
Canada 150
Australia 82

NICKEL (thousand tonnes)

China 1,210
USA 935
Russia 271

COAL (million tonnes)

▲ *The Mirniy diamond mine in Sakha republic. Diamonds are extracted from each terrace by opencast mining.*

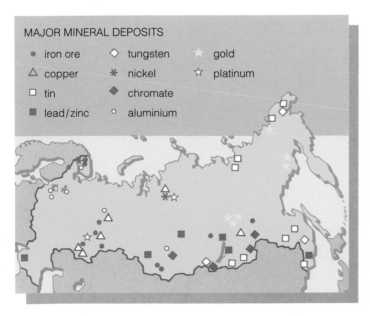

40.9 million tonnes in 1994, after China and the USA. Russia also occupied fourth place in the production of steel ingots in 1994, with 48.8 million tonnes, after Japan, China and the USA.

Gold is found in Siberia and in 1994 Russia was fourth in world production of the metal, with 147,000 kg, after South Africa, the USA and Australia.

Many of the valuable ores and minerals are located in the remote parts of Siberia and the Far East. Higher wages have to be paid to encourage people to work in these harsh environments — up to three times the average wages for similar jobs in Moscow. But spillages of oil and gas have caused considerable environmental damage. Many boggy areas in Siberia are contaminated with crude oil.

▲ *High-pressure steam hoses are used to melt the permafrost that overlies gas deposits in the Yamal Peninsula.*

▶ *The taiga has rich timber resources. Massive rafts made of felled logs are sent down rivers or across lakes to saw mills.*

MAJOR MINERAL DEPOSITS

- ● iron ore
- △ copper
- □ tin
- ■ lead/zinc
- ◇ tungsten
- ✳ nickel
- ◆ chromate
- ○ aluminium
- ★ gold
- ☆ platinum

POPULATION

NATIONALITIES

The last full census in Russia in 1989 listed 129 nationalities living in the territory. The Russians are the largest national grouping, with an estimated total population of 122 million in 1995. They belong to the European grouping known as the Slavs. Other Slav peoples living in Russia include Ukrainians and Belorussians. Over the years, members of all these groups have migrated to areas of Asiatic Russia too. In 1989, according to the census, the population of Russia's northern regions stood at 199,000, divided into 29 nationalities. These groups are obviously all very small: none of them makes up even

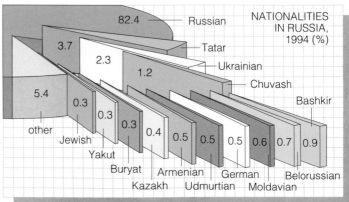

◀ *The Yakuts are the second largest native grouping in Siberia. They live in the coldest part of the region, and celebrate their summer festival by dancing, singing and feasting.*

NATIONALITIES IN RUSSIA, 1994 (%)

- 82.4 — Russian
- 3.7 — Tatar
- 2.3 — Ukrainian
- 1.2 — Chuvash
- Bashkir
- 5.4 — other
- 0.3 — Jewish
- 0.3 — Yakut
- 0.3 — Buryat
- 0.4 — Kazakh
- 0.5 — Armenian
- 0.5 — Udmurtian
- 0.5 — German
- 0.6 — Moldavian
- 0.7 — Belorussian
- 0.9 — Bashkir

0.1% of Russia's total population. The largest group is the Nentsy, with 34,000 members, while the smallest are the Entsi and the Oroki, with only about 200 each.

The lifestyles of people in Siberia and the Far East can be very different from those in European Russia, because of the cold

◀ ▼ *In the cities, most Russians live in tall blocks of flats. As housing can be scarce, the flats are small compared to British or US standards. One room may function as both a living room and a bedroom.*

KEY FACTS

● 30 million Russians have migrated to Siberia since the first settlers arrived in the 17th century.

● In 1994, the number of refugees and migrants in Russia increased from 447,933 to 702,451.

● Between January 1992 and January 1994, the population of Siberia fell by 89,000 and that of the Far East by 244,000.

● In 1994, there were 34 million women workers in Russia: 49% of the workforce.

● In 1994, 21 million pensioners were women: almost 3 times the number of male pensioners.

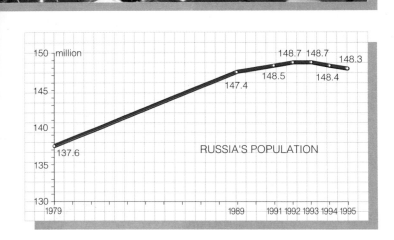

RUSSIA'S POPULATION

► *People in the Arctic areas must dress warmly, because of the extreme cold. These Nentsy children wear gloves, boots and hoods made of reindeer fur to protect themselves from the freezing winds.*

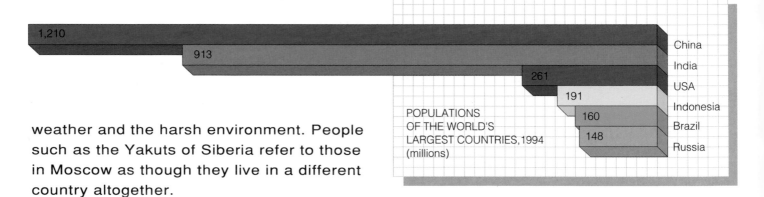

POPULATIONS OF THE WORLD'S LARGEST COUNTRIES, 1994 (millions)

China	1,210
India	913
USA	261
Indonesia	191
Brazil	160
Russia	148

weather and the harsh environment. People such as the Yakuts of Siberia refer to those in Moscow as though they live in a different country altogether.

THE CITIES

After the Second World War, as a result of rapid industrialization, many people moved from the countryside to the cities. The proportion of Russia's population living in towns and cities rose from 34% in 1945 to 52% in 1959; in 1994, the figure was 73%. This involved the migration of 40 million people, all in need of somewhere to live. The result was the building of tall blocks of flats in every major city in the country.

However, recently there has been a shift in the opposite direction. Between 1991 and 1995, Russia's urban population fell by 1.5 million, while the rural population increased by 1.3 million. One reason for this change is the difficulties of high living costs in Russian cities today: many food prices are similar to those in the shops of Britain and the USA, while in 1996 the wages of most working people were around 10% or less of the average in the UK and USA.

POPULATION LEVELS

Not only is the proportion of city dwellers declining, but Russia's overall population is falling too. The total number of people in the country fell by 300,000 in 1993 and by another 100,000 in 1994. The birth rate in 1994 stood at 9.6 per 1,000 people, down from 12.1 per 1,000 in 1991. The typical Russian family today has one or two children – although if a family has five or more children, the government presents the mother with a medal to honour her contribution to society.

The low birth rate is partly because of the cost of raising a family, even though the majority of Russian women work full-time. Although things are changing, it is also generally still the case that women are expected to do all the housework as well as working outside the home, so most women find it easier to have smaller families.

THE COUNTRYSIDE

People living in the villages still have very few services, apart from radio and television. Many have to go to the village well to fetch water for their everyday needs. A family normally keeps its own cow to supply milk, and chickens to provide eggs. People also grow their own fruits such as apples and cherries, and vegetables such as potatoes and onions.

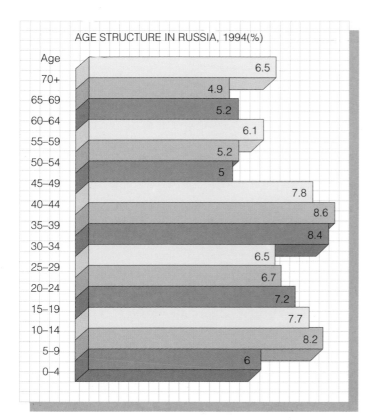

AGE STRUCTURE IN RUSSIA, 1994(%)

Age	%
70+	6.5
65–69	4.9
60–64	5.2
55–59	6.1
50–54	5.2
45–49	5
40–44	7.8
35–39	8.6
30–34	8.4
25–29	6.5
20–24	6.7
15–19	7.2
10–14	7.7
5–9	8.2
0–4	6

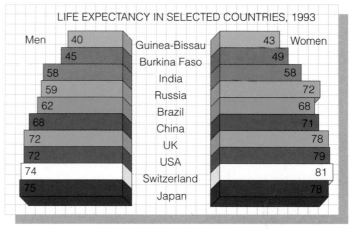

LIFE EXPECTANCY IN SELECTED COUNTRIES, 1993

Men	Country	Women
40	Guinea-Bissau	43
45	Burkina Faso	49
58	India	58
59	Russia	72
62	Brazil	68
68	China	71
72	UK	78
72	USA	79
74	Switzerland	81
75	Japan	78

▶ *Because of population movements, many Russians of European descent now live in Siberia and the Far East – like those pictured here, in Vladivostok.*

RELIGION

In the time of the USSR, schoolchildren were told that God did not exist. However, today many people in Russia do believe in God, and most of these belong to the Russian Orthodox Church. It has strict rules and rituals. For instance, it requires people to stand during the sermons, which can sometimes be quite long. Islam is the main religion in the southern republics of European Russia. Protestants and Buddhists are common in the Asiatic part of the country. Other religions include Catholicism and Judaism, but many Jewish people have moved to Israel since the late 1980s.

EDUCATION

Children start primary school at the age of 6 or 7 and leave at 10 or 11. Education is compulsory up to the age of 16, but many stay on until they are 18, when they may sit entrance examinations to reach a

FESTIVALS AND HOLIDAYS

January 1–2	NEW YEAR HOLIDAY
January 7	RUSSIAN ORTHODOX CHRISTMAS
February 23	RUSSIAN ARMY DAY
March 8	INTERNATIONAL WOMEN'S DAY
April 2	DAY OF THE UNITY OF THE PEOPLE
May 1–2	FIRST OF MAY DAY and WORKERS' SOLIDARITY DAY
May 9	VICTORY DAY
June 12	INDEPENDENCE DAY
November 7	RUSSIAN REVOLUTION HOLIDAY

▶ *A traditional wooden house, or "dacha", in the countryside. Many city dwellers have their own dachas, where they spend summer weekends or holidays and may grow fruit trees, green vegetables and potatoes. Home-made produce provides an important source of food for the winter.*

◀ *Drinking tea from a huge teapot, or "samovar". Once heated by burning coals inside them, most samovars today are powered by electricity.*

university or institute of higher education. At the age of 16, other students can go on to professional and technical schools where they learn special technical skills as entrance to a profession.

Some schools are now privately run, while others provide teaching in the language of one of Russia's many national groupings. There are also special language schools where several subjects are taught through the medium of one foreign language, and children also study the literature of the country concerned. The first "special English schools" opened in Moscow in the mid-1950s.

The school year runs from 1 September to the end of May or beginning of June, so Russian schoolchildren have long summer holidays. There are also three brief breaks in autumn, spring and the New Year.

KEY FACTS

● In 1992, 40 different religious denominations were registered in Russia.
● Most Russian schools teach English as a foreign language.
● In September 1994, 2.5 million students were enrolled in 553 higher institutes and universities.
● In 1993, there were 12,600 hospitals and clinics and 1 doctor for every 222 people (compared with 1 for every 611 people in the UK and 1 for every 395 in the USA).
● Every Russian citizen has to have an annual medical check-up.
● Children under 14 years old are not allowed to work.
● The standard working week is 40 hours long.
● Until the late 1980s, advertisements were not shown on Russian television.

▶ *Construction of the Moscow underground railway (metro) began in 1935. It now has 153 stations, connecting remote residential areas with the city centre. The Arbat metro station, shown here, is one of the oldest and most beautiful.*

▲ *There are many contrasts in modern Russia. This elderly woman is begging outside one of Moscow's most expensive stores.*

HEALTH

The health care system in Russia is free for everyone and includes the medical service of clinics and hospitals in each district of a city or rural area. Most schools also have a doctor or nurse. Medical aid is more difficult to obtain in the Arctic regions and in the remote areas of Siberia and the Far East. Helicopters are used to bring health professionals to these regions.

SPORT AND LEISURE

Sport is an everyday part of Russian life. It is compulsory at schools. Children train in the school gymnastic halls, outdoors and in the nearest swimming pools. Winter sports are popular in Russia and it is common for families to go skating or skiing at weekends. Hockey and figure skating are

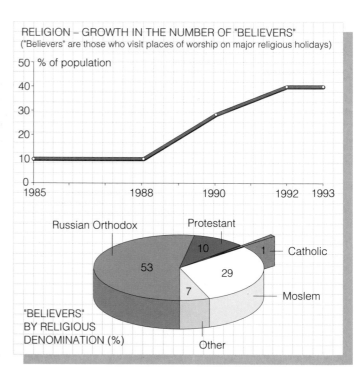

RELIGION – GROWTH IN THE NUMBER OF "BELIEVERS"
("Believers" are those who visit places of worship on major religious holidays)

50 % of population
40
30
20
10
0
1985   1988   1990   1992 1993

"BELIEVERS" BY RELIGIOUS DENOMINATION (%)

Russian Orthodox 53
Protestant 10
Catholic 1
Moslem 29
Other 7

◄ *The Moscow* PATRIARCH, *Alexei II, became head of the Russian Orthodox Church in 1988, when the church celebrated 1,000 years of Christianity in Russia.*

enjoyed by many, and Russia's hockey team and figure skaters are among the world's leaders. In summer, children often go to summer camps where they play all kinds of sports and leisure activities for a month or two. Football, volleyball and basketball are among the most popular summer sports.

Many Russians have a summer house, or "dacha", in the countryside where they spend weekends or summer holidays and where they grow fruit and vegetables.

Russian people like to celebrate holidays. They are very hospitable, inviting many guests home and treating them to lots of food. Birthdays are the favourite holidays, with New Year holidays not far behind. The most important person at New Year is Father Frost (similar to Santa Claus), who

is accompanied by his assistant, the Snowgirl. Russian Christmas is celebrated 13 days later than in Western Europe, because the Russian Orthodox Church operates according to the calendar in use in previous centuries. And because 30 million Russians died in the Second World War, Victory Day, celebrated on 9 May, is also an important date.

In recent years there have been many changes in the lives of Russian people. Some have become very rich, but others have become poor as prices for many goods have increased.

▼ *The school year starts on 1 September, when celebrations are held in schools and children bring flowers for their teachers.*

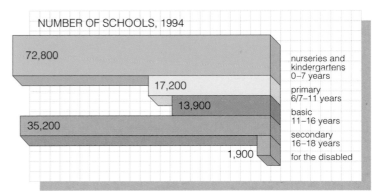

NUMBER OF SCHOOLS, 1994

72,800	nurseries and kindergartens 0–7 years
17,200	primary 6/7–11 years
13,900	basic 11–16 years
35,200	secondary 16–18 years
1,900	for the disabled

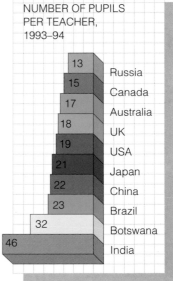

NUMBER OF PUPILS PER TEACHER, 1993–94

13	Russia
15	Canada
17	Australia
18	UK
19	USA
21	Japan
22	China
23	Brazil
32	Botswana
46	India

■ RULE AND LAW

◄ Britain's Queen Elizabeth II made her first visit to Russia in October 1994. She is shown here with President Boris Yeltsin and the Mayor of Moscow, Yuri Luzhkov.

► "Omon" is a special police force dealing with terrorism and criminal gangs. This Omon unit is holding a training exercise aimed at arresting a "suspect".

After the end of Communism in 1991, Russia established a Federal Assembly, which consists of two chambers. The upper chamber is called the Federation Council and has 178 nominated members. They do not serve for a fixed term, but continue for as long as they are re-elected as leaders in the regions. The lower chamber is called the State Duma and consists of 450 members; half are elected from party lists, while the other half are elected by the regions. The most powerful political figure is the President.

The Russian President is the head of state and commander of the armed forces, in much the same way as the President of the USA. He can issue presidential decrees on many subjects, such as defence, foreign policy and financial matters.

The Russian government is located in the

◄ The Russian emblem shows the two-headed eagle of the Tsars and an image of the patron saint, St George.

▼ The Russian flag.

KEY FACTS

● In June 1991, Boris Yeltsin was elected as the first President of the Russian Federation.
● In July 1996, he was re-elected for a second term.
● In December 1995, elections were held for the State Duma. The Russian Communist Party gained the largest number of seats.
● In January 1996, Russia joined the Council of Europe.
● In 1996, the Russian army consisted of 1.5 million soldiers. Almost all the ordinary soldiers are conscripts who serve for a minimum of 2 years.

capital, Moscow, and the President's office is in the Kremlin.

In each of Russia's 89 regions there is a presidential representative, a system that allows the President to stay in touch with the regions and keep informed about political issues.

The legal system reflects the great diversity of Russia's peoples, as each republic and region has its own court. The highest civil court is the Supreme Court of the Federation, located in Moscow.

The police forces of Russia are divided into three main groups. There are the frontier guards, who control entry to and exit from the country and protect the state's borders; the traffic police, who control roads both inside cities and between towns and cities; and the militia, who patrol the streets and deal with general issues relating to law and order and the civilian population.

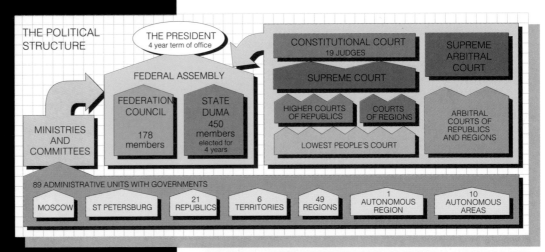

▶ *Women in the Chechnya republic protesting against the war there, which began in December 1994. The poster shows Chechen President Dudaev, who was killed in April 1996.*

FOOD AND FARMING

Farming in Russia highlights the very varied pattern of land use, due to the great variation in the country's climatic regions. Most of Russia's cultivated area forms a large triangular shape, with its base on the western border and the apex at Irkutsk in eastern Siberia. To the north of this area it is generally too cold to grow crops in the fields, although it is possible to cultivate crops in glasshouses. Because of the harsh climate and the long Russian winters, the cereal crops that do well are those that are known to be the most hardy. Russia is the world's leading producer of barley, oats and potatoes; but it is only the

▲ *Harvesting beetroot near Moscow. Agriculture in this region is primarily aimed at meeting the demands of its huge urban population.*

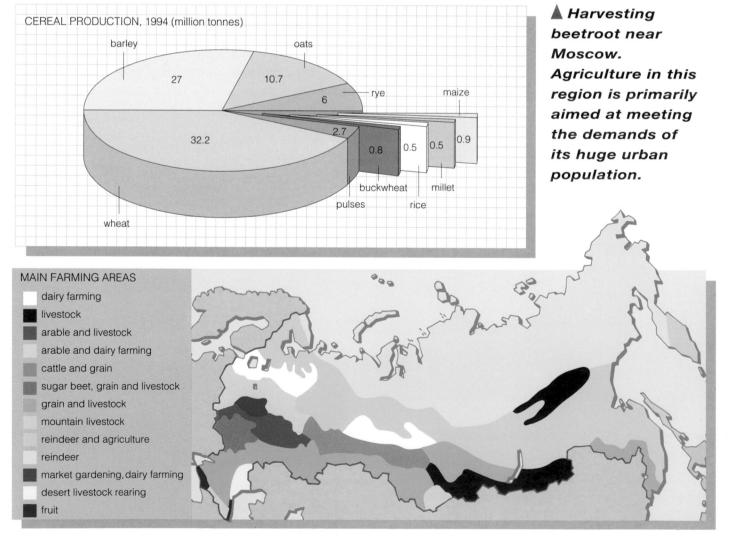

CEREAL PRODUCTION, 1994 (million tonnes)

barley 27
oats 10.7
rye 6
maize 0.9
wheat 32.2
pulses 2.7
buckwheat 0.8
rice 0.5
millet 0.5

MAIN FARMING AREAS
- dairy farming
- livestock
- arable and livestock
- arable and dairy farming
- cattle and grain
- sugar beet, grain and livestock
- grain and livestock
- mountain livestock
- reindeer and agriculture
- reindeer
- market gardening, dairy farming
- desert livestock rearing
- fruit

KEY FACTS

● In 1994, Russia had 29.4 million head of cattle, 17.6 million sheep and 14.5 million pigs.

● Food imports to Russia grew by 40% during 1995.

● Bread consumption by the average Russian is 3 times that of the average Briton or American.

● When the first McDonalds restaurant opened in Moscow in 1990, queues of 5,000 people formed outside. The cost of a burger and fries was equivalent to half an average day's wages.

● People who live in the Arctic north and Siberia often eat reindeer meat as part of their diet.

● In Siberia, people make hundreds of small meat dumplings called "pelmeni" and store them in the frozen ground in winter.

● Russia produces its own Soviet champagne, which is traditionally drunk on birthdays, weddings and holidays.

fourth largest producer of wheat. Its 1993 production of 42.5 million tonnes was less than half the total 105 million tonnes of the world's largest producer that year (China).

However, some parts of south European Russia and the areas near Vladivostok in the Far East have warm summers and good soils. Thus salad vegetables such as tomatoes and peppers can be grown, as well as fruits such as plums and watermelons. In the Russian Far East, soya beans are grown. Russians eat cereals that are rarely consumed in Britain or the USA. In particular, buckwheat is a popular choice. It is eaten with meat (usually pork or pork sausages) or is made into a porridge.

The poorer soils of north European Russia are suited to root vegetable production, especially cabbages and beetroot. These two vegetables form the

▶ *Russian workers and their families normally eat 3 hot meals a day. This family's supper consists of "zakuski", or appetizers, followed by chicken and a Russian favourite – buckwheat porridge.*

basis of the famous Russian soups which include meat and other vegetables and so are almost a meal in themselves. They are usually eaten at lunchtime. Cabbage soup is known as SHCHI and beetroot soup is called BORSHCH: sour cream is added when the soup is served and normally black rye bread accompanies the dish.

To preserve food for the long winter, Russians traditionally use methods such as pickling and salting. Pickled cucumbers and mushrooms are favourites, as are salted herrings, which may be served as a first course along with salad and salami sausage.

Russian breakfast can take several forms. It may consist of porridge made with oats or buckwheat, omelette or fried eggs, or Russian pancakes, known as BLINIS. Lunch can be eaten any time from noon to 4 pm, but is normally served around 1 pm to 2.30 pm. It often begins with a fish or meat salad, followed by soup, then meat and potatoes, sweet and coffee. Alternatively,

▲ *These combine harvesters are working together to bring in the wheat on the fertile Russian steppes. This is one of the largest collective farms in European Russia, covering 30,000 hectares.*

◄ *A rich harvest of red and yellow peppers is collected every year in the Stavropol region of southern Russia. Farmers also grow wheat, maize, sunflowers (for oil) and various fruits here. It is one of the country's most fertile areas.*

the main course might be fried or baked fish, chosen from a great variety of sea or river fish. Russia's most famous fish is the sturgeon, which lives in the Caspian Sea. It can weigh as much as 1 tonne and live for up to 75 years. The eggs, or roe, of the female sturgeon are canned as caviar, an expensive delicacy which is exported all over the world.

Because of the size of the country, Russian farms can be very large – up to 100,000 hectares. These were established by the former Soviet regime. All the farm workers jointly owned the crops and animals, so they were called "collective" farms. Animal collective farms specialize in rearing cattle, pigs, sheep or chickens. In the north of European Russia and Siberia, there are reindeer collective farms. Reindeer farming requires special skills, as the animals naturally migrate in search of food, so the farmers have to move with their reindeer. On the large cereal-producing farms of the steppes, teams of combine harvesters are needed to bring in the harvest.

There are also private farms in Russia – 280,000 of them in January 1996 – but these farmers own only 2% of the country's total agricultural land. More than half of private farmers own 20 hectares or less of land.

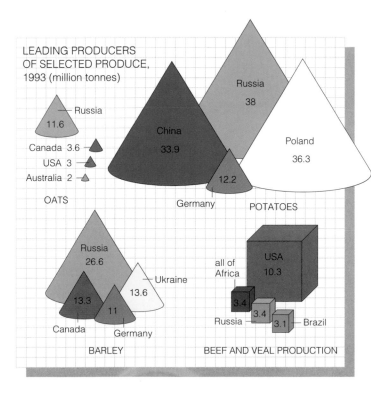

LEADING PRODUCERS OF SELECTED PRODUCE, 1993 (million tonnes)

Russia 11.6
Canada 3.6
USA 3
Australia 2
OATS

China 33.9
Russia 38
Poland 36.3
Germany 12.2
POTATOES

Russia 26.6
Canada 13.3
Germany 11
Ukraine 13.6
BARLEY

USA 10.3
all of Africa 3.4
Russia 3.4
Brazil 3.1
BEEF AND VEAL PRODUCTION

TRADE AND INDUSTRY

In 1994, industry employed 28% of
Russia's working population: this figure
has declined from a total of 30% in 1990.
Since Russian independence after the fall
of the Soviet Union in 1991, there have
been dramatic changes in the structure
of Russian industry. The country has
abundant natural resources, including oil,
natural gas and coal, so mineral products
form a significant part of its exports.

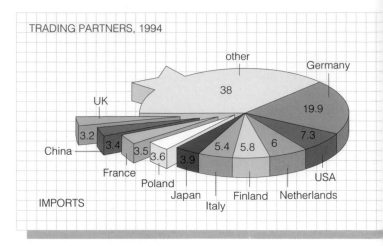

TRADING PARTNERS, 1994

other 38
Germany 19.9
7.3
USA
Netherlands 6
Finland 5.8
Italy 5.4
Japan 3.9
Poland 3.6
France 3.5
China 3.4
UK 3.2

IMPORTS

◀ *An assembly
line of lorries in
Naberezhniye
Chelny, Tatarstan
republic. The
"Kamaz" lorries
built here are
among the best-
known in Russia.*

▶ *Magnitogorsk's
metallurgical
works is the
largest in Russia.
It produced 15.9
million tonnes of
steel in 1993.*

MANUFACTURING

The proportion of people employed in
manufacturing fell from 83% of the total
workforce in 1990 to 53% in 1994, while the
proportion of those working in the private
sector grew from 12.5% to 33% in the same
period. This reflects the scale of recent
privatization: the private sector of the economy
now produces 25% of Russia's wealth.

The iron and steel industry remains
important, and the country is the world's

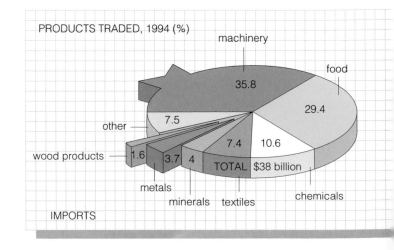

PRODUCTS TRADED, 1994 (%)

machinery 35.8
food 29.4
chemicals 10.6
textiles 7.4
minerals 4
metals 3.7
wood products 1.6
other 7.5
TOTAL $38 billion

IMPORTS

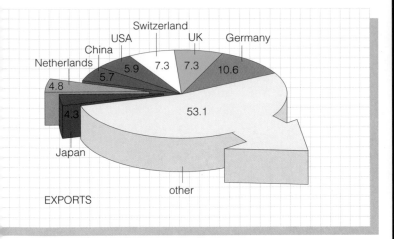

Switzerland
USA
China
Netherlands
Germany
UK
5.9
7.3
7.3
10.6
5.7
4.8
4.3
53.1
Japan
other

EXPORTS

KEY FACTS

● In 1994, Russia exported 3,258,000 tonnes of steel and 2,301,000 tonnes of aluminium.
● Exports of cars fell from 396,000 in 1992 to 207,000 in 1994.
● Machinery and machine tools form Russia's largest category of imports, totalling US$ 10,667 million in 1994.
● In December 1994, about 129,000 foreign workers were employed in Russia.
● In December 1995, 6 million people in Russia were out of work: 8.2% of the working population.
● Unemployment benefit in Russia normally lasts for only 6 months.

third largest producer of pig iron and the fourth most important producer of steel. Major industrial centres are located around Moscow in the European part of the country, in the Urals industrial region and in south Siberia, in an area known as the Kuznetsk basin or Kuzbass (centred on the city of Novokuznetsk).

Car and lorry manufacturing is located in Moscow and at Tol'yatti on the River Volga. In 1993, Russia produced 956,000 private cars, 526,000 motorcycles and 1.7 million trolley buses. Some 89,000 tractors were manufactured for agricultural use, along with 33,000 combine harvesters.

FOREIGN TRADE

In 1994, Russian exports were worth almost twice the cost of the country's imports, with exports valued at US$ 64 billion, compared with US$ 38 billion in imports.

Russia's trade is conducted mainly with European countries, with Germany in the primary position for both imports and exports. Other important partners are China and Japan. Household goods such

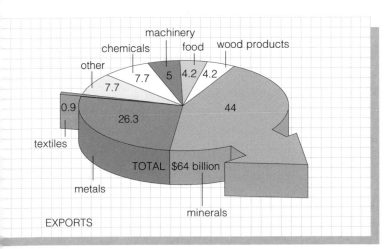

machinery
chemicals
food
wood products
other
7.7
5
4.2
4.2
7.7
0.9
44
26.3
textiles
TOTAL $64 billion
metals
minerals

EXPORTS

as kitchen utensils from China and Japan are found in Russian shops. The USA also trades with Russia, and Russia imports more from the USA than it exports. Machinery, machine parts and food form the main basis of Russian imports, while minerals and metals are the basis of its exports. In 1994, Russia exported 92,000 tonnes of crude oil and 39,000 tonnes of refined oil and oil products. Natural gas exports totalled 109 billion cubic metres, making Russia the world's leading exporter of natural gas.

TRAVEL AND TOURISM

There have been recent fluctuations in the structure and statistics of travel to and from Russia. The number of foreign visitors fell from 5.4 million in 1993 to 3.3 million in 1994, although the proportion of those who were tourists remained the same, at 28% each year. However, in 1995 the number of

▲ *The Labyrinth company is jointly owned by Russian, British and Austrian firms and has several trading halls in Moscow. It is one of many joint ventures in Russia today.*

visitors rose to 5.2 million. Russia expects a tourist boom by the year 2000, with a projected 15 million people visiting the country annually. Meanwhile, the number of Russians travelling abroad increased from 8.5 million in 1993 to 9.1 million in 1994, with the proportion of those who were tourists rising from 19% to 28%.

The neighbouring states of Estonia and Lithuania were the top two destinations for Russians travelling abroad in 1994. Next came Turkey, which is popular for shopping trips. Nearly three times as many Russians visited the USA compared with the number of Americans who travelled to Russia, while

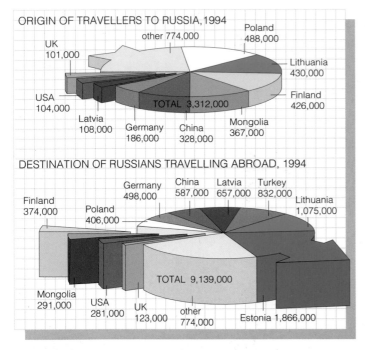

ORIGIN OF TRAVELLERS TO RUSSIA, 1994

other 774,000
Poland 488,000
UK 101,000
Lithuania 430,000
USA 104,000
Finland 426,000
TOTAL 3,312,000
Latvia 108,000
Germany 186,000
China 328,000
Mongolia 367,000

DESTINATION OF RUSSIANS TRAVELLING ABROAD, 1994

Germany 498,000
China 587,000
Latvia 657,000
Turkey 832,000
Finland 374,000
Poland 406,000
Lithuania 1,075,000
TOTAL 9,139,000
Mongolia 291,000
USA 281,000
UK 123,000
other 774,000
Estonia 1,866,000

similar numbers of Britons and Russians visited each others' country.

THE RETAIL SECTOR

Since 1992, there has been a great increase in the variety and choice of consumer goods that are available in large Russian cities. More than 250 supermarkets have opened in Moscow. Western brands of toothpaste and chocolate bars are among the most popular imported items.

▼ *GUM, one of Russia's oldest department stores, is in Moscow. Following refurbishment in 1991, it stocks numerous foreign products.*

▬ TRANSPORT

Transport is a major problem in Russia, because of the sheer size of the country and the diversity of its landscape.

Russia has the longest railway in the world, covering 9,332 km between Moscow and Vladivostok, running across East Europe and Siberia. It is known as the Trans-Siberian railway. Construction work on the line began more than a century ago, in 1892. It takes six days to complete the journey, and trains can sometimes be as much as 24 hours late.

The second Siberian railway, built between 1974 and 1985, is known as the Baikal–Amur Mainline, or BAM. It takes part of its name from the famous Siberian Lake Baikal. The line is 3,145 km long, of which more than 2,000 km are laid on permafrost. In spring, when the ice from the permafrost melts, there can be major problems: features known as icings bend and distort the track and make for an expensive repair job.

The road network is concentrated in European Russia and extends to eastern Siberia. Most of these roads were built between 1928 and 1950. There is no continuous road across the eastern parts of the country, although there is a separate route in the Far East called the Aldan highway. A motorway between St Petersburg and Nizhniy Novgorod, via Moscow, is currently being built and is due to open in 1998.

In January 1995, there were 12.4 million private cars in Russia – compared with 21.1 million in the UK, whose population is two and a half times less. The most popular model is the Lada, while the most popular

◄ *Russia's icebreakers clear the way for cargo ships after the long Arctic winter. This one, in the Kara Sea, has the old Soviet symbols (hammer and sickle) on its funnel.*

MODES OF TRANSPORT, 1994 (million tonnes of freight)

rail 1,058
road 1,931
pipeline 801
other 62.1
ships 6.9
air 1
waterways 155
TOTAL 4,015

KEY FACTS

● In 1994, Russia had 743,000 km of paved roads, compared with 6.24 million km in the USA and 377,873 km in the UK.

● There are 94,000 km of inland waterways and 87,000 km of rail track.

● People pay a flat fare to travel any distance on the Moscow or St Petersburg metros.

● As of January 1996, there were also metro systems in 4 other Russian cities.

● Public transport is free for pensioners.

● Russia has 110 major airports and there are also more than 120 air strips in the north and Siberia.

● Russia has 41 major sea ports.

● Car imports totalled 182,461 in 1993, but this fell to 60,653 in 1994.

● Buying a car in Russia means making payment in full at the time purchase is agreed – no credit system is available.

▲ Helicopters are the only reliable form of transport during the Arctic winter in remote settlements such as here, on the Chukotka Peninsula in the Far East.

▼ The River Moskva is used by commercial shipping, such as these barges, along most of its course.

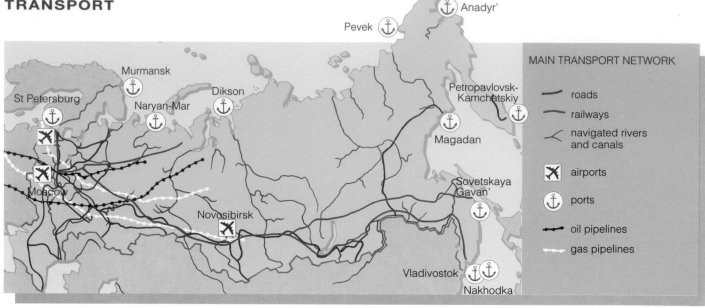

MAIN TRANSPORT NETWORK

— roads

— railways

⟨ navigated rivers and canals

✈ airports

⚓ ports

●—● oil pipelines

○—○ gas pipelines

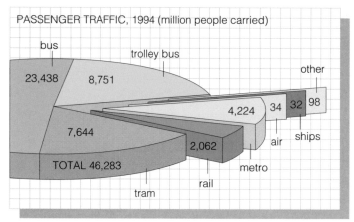

PASSENGER TRAFFIC, 1994 (million people carried)

bus 23,438

trolley bus 8,751

7,644

2,062

TOTAL 46,283

tram

rail

metro

4,224

air 34

ships 32

other 98

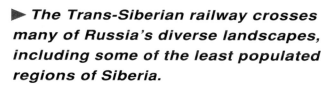

▶ **The Trans-Siberian railway crosses many of Russia's diverse landscapes, including some of the least populated regions of Siberia.**

imported model is the Volvo, from Sweden.

Pipelines form another important part of the transport network. They are used to transport oil and natural gas.

In the northern parts of Russia, especially Siberia, air transport is often the only means of moving people and goods. Helicopters are used in the remote areas, as they do not require a runway and can land on snow and ice without difficulty. The Russian national airline is called Aeroflot. Since 1990 it has been divided into separate companies, and by 1995 there

were more than 50 of these. The airlines now seen at European airports, along with Aeroflot, are usually Russian International Airlines and Transaero.

For many years the Russians have attempted to develop a sea route along the Arctic coast: this is usually known as the Northern Sea route. In spite of the use of modern icebreakers, the harsh environment here still causes problems. For example, in October 1983 the eastern part of the Arctic Ocean froze solid and trapped seven ships for nearly six months.

THE ENVIRONMENT

◄ *The oil industry has created many environmental problems. This oil leak at Usinsk in 1994 took months to clean up.*

▼ *Once common in European Russia, brown bears are now found chiefly in Siberia and the Far East. In 1994, there were 125,800 of them.*

Russia's various regions have different environmental problems and advantages.

European Russia has a very long history of economic development. As a result, more than half of its old forests have been cut down over the last three centuries, and animal life has been depleted. Recent attempts to remedy this have included reintroducing certain species, such as European bisons, which are now protected.

Central regions, including Moscow, have serious problems with water and air pollution. In the southern part of European Russia, huge dams built on the River Volga have blocked the way to the traditional spawning grounds of the precious sturgeon.

Unique European antelopes called "saigas" still graze on the steppes of Kalmykia near the Caspian Sea, as they have since ancient times. But the raising of too many sheep and cattle has destroyed the fragile sandy soils and created a desert here.

As Siberia and the Far East are more sparsely populated, there are fewer overall

NATURE RESERVES AND NATIONAL PARKS

- · nature reserves less than 100,000 hectares
- ● nature reserves greater than 100,000 hectares
- ☐ national parks

▶ *The Amur or Ussurian tiger lives in the forests of the southern Far East. Although it is a protected species, some animals can be seen in zoos across the world. Recently, its numbers have declined because of poaching.*

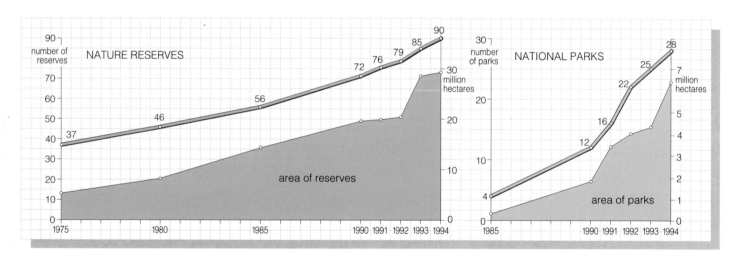

problems. But in some places, the oil, natural gas and coal industries have had an adverse impact. Tundra landscapes are very fragile, as it takes 70 years for reindeer moss to grow to its normal height of just a few centimetres. Over the last 30 years, more than 6 million hectares of reindeer pasture have been destroyed by the effects of the oil and gas industries.

There are more than 1,400 species of plant and animal life in Lake Baikal. More than half are unique, including the scaleless deep-water Golomyanka fish and the world's only freshwater seal. But industry poses threats here, too. A pulp and paper plant at Baikalsk has been polluting the lake for more than 30 years, despite the opposition of environmentalists.

Siberian forests have always been rich in fur-bearing animals such as sable, used to

decorate the British Queen's coronation robes. There are also mink, ermine, polecats, polar and silver foxes and squirrels here. Large mammals such as elk live in the taiga too, and there is one elk-raising farm in European Russia.

In the south of the Far East, there are unique contrasting landscapes known as "Ussurian taiga" where northern and southern species of trees grow together, including the Siberian larch and Mongolian oak. Both brown and black bears live here, as do snow leopards and Amur tigers, while the Japanese thrush is one of the numerous species of birds.

Despite its problems, Russia has one of the world's best systems of protected areas. About 15% of its territory, mainly in Siberia, is untouched by humans. Throughout the country there are nature reserves, where people are only allowed to visit for purposes of study. National parks are also popular with tourists.

KEY FACTS

● Russian forests cover 771.1 million hectares, or 45% of the total territory.
● In 1994, more than half a million hectares of forests were destroyed in 20,000 fires.
● Transport is responsible for two-thirds of air pollution in Moscow. During rush hours, emissions are 3 times greater than the maximum permitted level.
● Since 1978, the level of the Caspian Sea has risen by more than 2 metres, bringing the threat of flooding.
● More than 8,000 sq km of Russian land are still contaminated by radiation, 10 years after the accident at Chernobyl (Ukraine) in 1986.

■ THE FUTURE

◄ *Moscow's Cathedral of Christ the Saviour is a symbol of recent changes. After the 1917 Revolution, it was demolished and replaced by a swimming pool. Work on its reconstruction began in January 1995, and it was completed in just 12 months – a full 4 years ahead of schedule.*

► *The Arbat is a fashionable area in central Moscow which has always been popular with writers and artists. It now has a McDonalds restaurant as well.*

Despite many environmental and economic problems, Russia's economy is growing and inflation has slowed down. With a wealth of natural resources and a well-educated labour force, Russia has great potential.

Emphasis on the development of mineral-rich regions in Siberia and the Far East is expected to continue, using existing railways and roads and building new ones jointly with Western companies. Exchange of technologies will involve sharing the unique approach to eye surgery developed by Russian doctors, and an influx of

KEY FACTS

● About 3–5% of the population have an annual income of more than £80,000/US$120,000. They are known as "New Russians".

● In 1997, Moscow celebrates its 850th anniversary. Russia's first underground shopping complex will open in the city.

● By the middle of the 21st century, about 75% of all passenger air travel will be routed across Russia and the North Pole.

● Russia's agricultural system has been transformed. The country is likely to become an exporter of cereals by the year 2005.

Western technologies into Russia. Current joint efforts include research into how to help children affected by the Chernobyl disaster.

An agreement signed with Belarus, Kazakhstan and Kyrgyzstan in 1996 shows that Russia is forging closer links with the former Soviet republics. It is also more open to the world economy and its share of exports to Western Europe and North America is set to grow.

As Russia has become less militarized, strategic regions in the Arctic areas that have been closed to international air traffic will be opened up. This will dramatically alter global travel routes, saving time by linking North America with Eurasia via the North Pole.

There is a long-term plan to build a channel under the 80-km Bering Strait that divides Eurasia and North America and to construct a railway through it. This will make the division of the world into East and West meaningless. It is also hoped to build a transcontinental highway from Western Europe via Russia into North America.

Since 1991, more Russians have been able to travel to foreign countries and more people from abroad have visited Russia. This trend continues to open up the country to new ideas and influences, particularly among the younger generation.

▶ *In 1991, a millionaires' club was formed in Moscow. Today there are many billionaires in the country too. Ilya Mitkov, pictured here, is one of the youngest of them.*

FURTHER INFORMATION

- RUSSIAN TOURIST INFORMATION SERVICE
219 Marsh Wall, London E14 9PD
(Provides information on Russia's regions)
- THE BRITAIN-RUSSIA CENTRE
The East-West Centre, 14 Grosvenor Place,
London SW1X 7HW
(Library open to the public by appointment)
- THE SCHOOL OF SLAVONIC AND
EAST EUROPEAN STUDIES
Senate House, Malet Street, London WC1E 7HU
(Library open to the public, for a fee)

BOOKS ABOUT RUSSIA

Focus on Russia and the Republics,
Elizabeth Roberts, Evans 1992 (age 9–12)
Russia, David Cumming, Wayland 1994
(age 9–12)
The Russian Federation, David Flint,
Franklin Watts 1992 (age 9–12)
Russian Food and Drink, Valentina
Lapenkova and Edward Lambton,
Wayland 1987 (age 11+)

GLOSSARY

BLINI
A Russian pancake made with wheat flour
and served with minced meat or jam.

BORSHCH
Pronounced "borshuss". Russian beetroot
soup with meat, potato, carrot, onion and
cabbage, served with sour cream.

CHERNOZEM
An extremely fertile, black-coloured soil,
with a rich organic top layer which may be
more than 1 metre deep.

COMMUNISM
An economic and political system in which
private ownership is abolished and all
industry is controlled by the state. The
Soviet Union was a Communist state
until 1991.

PATRIARCH
Head of the Russian Orthodox Church and
the spiritual leader of Russian Christians.

PERMAFROST
A layer of permanently frozen earth in
Russia's north and across most of Siberia.
It has remained frozen since the end of
the last Ice Age and can be 1–800 metres
thick.

PRIVATIZATION
The process of selling state-owned
factories and shops to private individuals
or groups of shareholders. In Russia, this
process started in 1992 and was virtually
complete by December 1995.

SHCHI
Pronounced "sheee". A thick cabbage soup
with meat, onion, garlic, potato and carrot,
served with sour cream.

STEPPE
A landscape of tall grasses, resistant to
drought and frost, with a few shrubs along
river valleys. The steppe forms the major
wheat-growing areas of Russia.

TAIGA
The area of coniferous forest which
stretches from the western border of Russia
across Siberia and the Far East. It forms
the largest forest in the world.

TSAR
The title of the Russian monarchs who ruled
from 1547 to 1917.

TUNDRA
The treeless landscape north of the taiga.
It consists of mosses, sedges and shrubs.

INDEX

ARCTIC
OCEAN

75°
60°
45°
30°
15°
0°
15°
30°
45°

75° 60° 45° 30° 15° 0° 15° 30° 45° 60° 75° 90° 105° 120° 135° 150° 165° 180° 165° 150° 135° 120° 105° 90° 75°

NORWAY

DEN.

SWEDEN

FINLAND

BALTIC SEA

ESTONIA

LATVIA

LITHUANIA

POLAND

KALININGRAD
OBLAST

BELARUS

MOLDOVA

UKRAINE

BLACK
SEA

KARACHAEVO-
CHERKESSIA

ADYGEYA

KABARDINO-
BALKARIA

NORTH
OSSETIA

INGUSHETIYA

GEORGIA

ARMENIA

AZERBAIJAN

TURKEY

St Petersburg

KARELIA

BARENTS
SEA

KARA
SEA

YAMAL PENINSULA

Arkhangel'sk

Usinsk

KOMI

RUSSIAN

MOSCOW

Nizhniy Novgorod

Kursk

MARI

UDMURTIA

MORDOVIA

TATARSTAN

Naberezhniye Chelny

CHUVASHIA

BASHKORTOSTAN

Yekaterinburg

Tol'yatti

Samara

Chelyabinsk

Volgograd

Magnitogorsk

Omsk

Novosibirsk

Novokuznetsk

Stavropol

CHECHNYA

KALMYKIA

DAGESTAN

CASPIAN SEA

KAZAKHSTAN

GORNO-
ALTAI

IRAN

TURKMENISTAN

UZBEKISTAN

KYRGYZSTAN